Harry and the Dinosaurs Like ...

Based on the original classic Harry and the Dinosaurs stories
written by Ian Whybrow, illustrated by Adrian Reynolds
Adapted by Catherine Baker

Harry and the dinosaurs like to swim.

They like to swim a lot!

Harry and the dinosaurs like to run.

They like to run a lot!

Harry and the dinosaurs like to cook.

They like to cook a lot!

Harry and the dinosaurs
like to go RAAAAH!